Alone at the Border

poems by

Albert Tacconelli

Finishing Line Press
Georgetown, Kentucky

Alone at the Border

*Alone at the Border is poetry inspired by
the horrific images I have seen on the internet of
our devastated Syrian sisters and brothers.
May these poems hasten the blessings of peace
for this ancient and violated land.*

Copyright © 2018 by Albert Tacconelli
ISBN 978-1-63534-662-6 First Edition
All rights reserved under International and Pan-American Copyright Conventions. No part of this book may be reproduced in any manner whatsoever without written permission from the publisher, except in the case of brief quotations embodied in critical articles and reviews.

ACKNOWLEDGMENTS

Publisher: Leah Maines
Editor: Christen Kincaid
Cover Art: iStock.com/Monik-a
Author Photo: Ronald Howard
Cover Design: Elizabeth Maines McCleavy

Printed in the USA on acid-free paper.
Order online: www.finishinglinepress.com

Author inquiries and mail orders:
Finishing Line Press
P. O. Box 1626
Georgetown, Kentucky 40324
U. S. A.

Table of Contents

Alone at the Border

Alone at the Border 1
How Where If 2
Too Late No Escape 3
Cold Hands 4
Their World 5
Huddle in Rubble 6
What Grief 7
Swept Away 8

Perhaps Something

Perhaps Something 9
Cautiously 10
With or Without 11
Hop Skip Jump 12
This is Syria 13
Pagliaccio's 14

Ad Nauseam

Ad Nauseam 15
Tell Me 16
So Close 17
Expedience 18
Completed Burial 19
Memorial 20
Unknown Brother 21

White Tents

White Tents 22
Together in the Rain 23
Four Wings 24
My Son Remembers 25
Music Unheard 26
Look for Me 27
Abandoned 28
Enough 29
Little Sparrow 30

...all that was dear to us is laid waste.
Can you hold back, O Lord, after all this?
Can you remain silent, and afflict us so severely?

—Isaiah 64:3,1

Soli Sancto Spiritui

Alone at the Border

Alone at the Border

In parched desolation, do borders matter?
Everywhere crushed water bottles lie scattered;
those who stayed, those who moved on.

Seated on a suitcase, exhausted from heat,
weary young man rests bowed head on his hand;
the world, one suitcase and the desert.

What will become of this refugee fleeing Syria?
Family is dead, friends lost among nations;
alone at the border is not easy.

Alone at the Border

How Where If

Young Syrian couple, two small sons live
among thousands of other refugee families.
Many harsh miles in their journey remain.
Who cares how, where, or if they arrive?

Too late. No escape.

Sudden air strikes
destroyed buildings,
decimated lives.

Trapped beneath
tons of concrete
the paralyzed youth
reached for life.

Whose hands lifted
fallen concrete?
Whose eyes met
his unblinking eyes?

It was finished,
the youth died
before he died.
Too late. No escape.

Alone at the Border

Cold Hands

Blood stained sheet,
two children sleep.

Cold hands touch,
reassure one another;
Yes, in the morning,
nightmare passed,
Mother will wake us.

But, no parent, no one
rouses the dead from sleep.

O suffering Syria
parents weep; sons,
daughters drown
in their own blood.
Who hears the cry?

Their World

The fine steady rain,
pinnacled white tents
surround two little boys
making their way home.

Who is home
waiting for refugee
children born hearing
bombs exploding;
playmates, neighbors
vanishing in dust?

Two little boys,
two little brothers
hold on to each other;
after all, brother's blood
is thicker than water.
The world is still theirs.

Alone at the Border

Huddle in Rubble

Two children huddle in rubble,
the little girl's arm and hand
rest on younger brother's head;
he peeks out, she hides her
face from a world gone mad.

Alone, clinging to each other,
no sheltering embrace,
bombed city without shelter;
parents, playmates, neighbors—
blood stains remain.

O Syria, once lovely,
who comes to your aid?

What Grief

See, the weeping father
cradles the Christ child
swathed in blood.

What grief like the father's grief,
insanely murdered son?
See hands, feet, trousers soaked red.

What grief like the refugee's grief
fleeing beheadings, hangings,
massacred martyred corpses?

O Syria, once lovely.
O Syria, tears of blood.
O Syria, madness without end.

Alone at the Border

Swept Away

Asleep on a curb in huge Istanbul,
the child lies across the wretched
father's lap—passersby ignore
refugees pleading for compassion.
The indifferent remain well fed.
The well fed remain indifferent.

Soon, winter and starvation will
sweep away the frozen dead—
rubbish from a dirty street.

Perhaps Something

Perhaps Something

Misty dust fills the sky, obscures
mountains, hovers ruin upon ruin—
neighborhoods once boisterous,
marketplaces once vibrant.

Families, friends, neighbors search
endless heaps of destruction,
hopeless to find any living thing,
even frightened pet cat or dog.

Perhaps something familiar will be found;
tatter of cloth, splinter of furniture.
Surely buried beneath crumpled
concrete, plaster and twisted steel
lie scattered scraps of loved ones lost.

Through indiscriminate catastrophe
stunned Syrians wend their slow way,
wondering how to create new life
where little that lives survives.

Perhaps Something

Cautiously

Stepping cautiously
through rubbled streets,
stricken neighbors
search for the dead;
in bloodied puddles
they find body parts.

With or Without

Distant city's crowded buildings
look like jumbled sugar cubes; from
the city flows a wide drainage channel
accumulating fetid sewage,
accumulating bloated corpses.

Along sloping sides of concrete walls
the apprehensive search for their dead.
With or without pity, the retrieved
will be wrapped in white sheets;
scribbled names or nothing to identify.

Deep in burial pits they will lie,
row upon row, white bundles of laundry
waiting for Syrian soil to cover them.

Perhaps Something

Hop Skip Jump

The barefoot boy leaps high
above rumpled rows of nightmares;
above rumpled rows of corpses.

The leaping boy banishes bad dreams
far away; a lonely beach—deceased aunts,
uncles, cousins glisten like pebbles.

Lonely beach, temporary morgue—
brief resting place before deep trenches
grow deeper, more dreadful with losses.

This is Syria,

five orphaned boys
blanched with bloody tears,
nostrils and lives
clogged with dust—
five cauterized souls.

Look into forgotten eyes.
Whose heart will open—
embrace five fragments
of frightened humanity?
O orphaned Syria.

Perhaps Something

Pagliaccio's

face is pale,
powdered with ash;
mascaraed eyes,
smudged with blood.

Pagliaccio's costume,
blood splattered flesh;
the empty stage,
covered with dust.

Among the ruins
Pagliaccio vanishes.
O lonely Syria.

Ad Nauseam

Ad Nauseam

Air strikes come and go.
Flames consume vehicles
ad nauseam.

Seeking safety and aid
three fleeing Syrians
carry a wounded comrade.

The dead and the dying
litter roadsides, gutters,
heaped on piles of rubble.

Foreign correspondents ask
questions, demand answers
ad nauseam.

Ad Nauseam

Tell Me

Stray bullets
punctured my chest,
flying shrapnel
slashed my guts.
Tell me, Doctor,
will I live?

So Close

Bloodied gloves
cupped the fractured,
gauze-wrapped head.

What medic could save
so blood soaked a soul
so close to death?

O wounded Syria,
so close to death,
who hears your cry?

Ad Nauseam

Expedience

Call it expedience of war—
trench hardly deep enough
to cram the dead youth, no time
to ponder the moment's solemnity.

They flee for their lives broken-hearted,
abandon the young Syrian soldier
whose warm body would soon grow cold.

On a day of peace free men will return,
with dignity pour libations of tears—
honor the unforgotten comrade.

Completed Burial

Comrades fled the shallow grave;
the dead soldiers' stiff hands protruded
from camouflaged uniform's sleeves.

O irrevocable death—my tears,
solemn prayers, irrational oaths
did not restore the brief life.
Shovelful by shovelful
I completed the burial,
concealed exposed hands,
lest the enemy, seeing the body,
wreak sacrilege—exhume,
drench with petrol,
ignite a flaming spectacle.

Syria's withered flower blooms
forever in heaven's garden;
parents, family, friends
grieve their grievous loss.

Ad Nauseam

Memorial

Whose soldier's head is this concealed
beneath hooded uniform's raised collar?
Whose soldier's lifeless hands dangle
from camouflaged uniform's sleeves?

Into barely wide, quickly dug trench,
the warm body is hastily wedged—
freed from whining bullets' stings,
freed from death's winged surprise.

Fallen to his knees, the Syrian soldier dies.
Bloody puddle forms a protecting moat
around the youth who died for the country
where he was born, is buried.

Unknown Brother

Wretched man,
brother of my humanity.
What did you do,
head battered, mauled with blood?
What could you have done
to die so brutally?
What crime so grave
to warrant such a death?

Unknown brother,
alone in the burning sun,
strapped to the metal crossbar—
around your sagging torso
the bloodied sign scribbled in
Arabic is nonsense, unless your
humiliated life proclaimed
crucified by lunacy.

Would that I could,
sever the leather straps,
lower you gently in my arms,
cleanse clotted flesh,
wrap bruised body
in white cotton sheet—
stand over your grave
and weep.

White Tents

White Tents

The mother,
what does she see?
White UN tents.
And beyond white UN tents,
what does the mother see?
Snow on the mountains?
Endless rows of families
living like nomads.

The mother waits
for husband, family, friends.
On the mother's lap a child sits
quietly wondering
why the world is white tents,
brilliant white tents,
crenulated sea of white tents.

Together in the Rain

walking the highway,
my little girl and I flee
Syria for safety,
perhaps to Lebanon.

My little girl and I
together, walking
the rainy highway,
I kiss her tears away.

White Tents

Four Wings

Futile fleeing ceased, mother and son
lay motionless on their backs—
rolled blanket carried few belongings,
son's foot rested gently on callused foot.

Was it stray bullets killed the mother,
the little boy? I see no wounds,
no trickles of dried blood.
Was it in Syria's hot dusty air
poisoned gas stole last gasps away?

Four arms, four wings spread wide
soar high above Syria,
safe from harm, eternally at peace.

My Son Remembers

I hold my son close,
not the faintest smile.
We live for his smiles.

My son remembers
daily bombs overhead
sounding like thunder.

My son remembers
our house, our friends
before thunder fell.

My son knows
we can't go back.

White Tents

Music Unheard

Carefully to her son's puckering
mouth she lifts the plastic spoon;
distant music distracts the child.

Softly the mother whispers;
eat, grow strong, become a man—
in a world made mad by

misguided youths, dying,
creating a phony world without heart,
without compassion?

Forgotten, the far away music
heard on their mother's lap—
music unheard since by anyone.

Look for Me

If anyone says,
Look, he is there;
look, he is in the desert.

Do not believe them.
I am near.

I am the forgotten
lives of the displaced.
Look for me.

Abandoned

I am a child,
no coaxed smile for
the journalist's camera.

I am a child, half-clothed,
head wrapped with gauze;
explosions, confusion—
I lost my parents.

I am one million orphans
scattered throughout Syria,
the Middle East—we are
everywhere, abandoned.

I am a child.
I am alone.
Will you help me?

Enough

No Room, anywhere.
Crowded, everywhere.
Go away, they say.

I say, look at my son.
See how sweet his face—
without a place to sleep.

The night is cold.
Donkey, oxen
huddle for warmth—

for mother and child,
hot breath of donkey
and oxen are enough.

Help nurse my infant.
Give me a little bread,
my breasts will make milk.

Perhaps this inn
there will be room.
Yousef has gone to ask.

White Tents

Little Sparrow

I found the little sparrow
fallen among debris,
so frightened, she
allowed me to feel
her heart's fast beating.
God loves sparrows,
knows sparrows by
name; my name, too.

With a shriek birds
flee across the sky,
people are silent,
my blood aches from waiting.

—Mehmed Mesa Selimovic

Albert Tacconelli's poetry appears in such journals as: *Paterson Literary Review; Philadelphia Poets; Endicott Review; VIA;* and is represented in anthologies: *Avanti Popolo: Italian-Americans Writers Sailing Beyond Columbus; Poetry Ink Tenth, Thirteenth, Fourteenth, Sixteenth, Twentieth Anniversary Anthologies; Moonstone Poetry Series 2015 Anthology of Featured Poets; American Italian Historical Association: Italian Americans and the Arts & Culture; American Italian Historical Association: We've Always Been Here; Edward Albert Maruggi's Remembrances: Humorous Happenings While Traveling in Italy. The American Voice in Poetry: Legacy of Whitman, Williams, and Ginsberg.* Featured poet of the month, on line newsletter; *a muse: janet mason*; and heard on the radio program, *Around The Kitchen Table*, MAR, 1540 AM. Bordighera Press (2014) published the first collection of poetry, *Perhaps Fly*. Passaic County Community College has exhibited Tacconelli's art works. Several paintings, prints, and drawings are included in the Permanent Collection of Contemporary Art.

www.ingramcontent.com/pod-product-compliance
Lightning Source LLC
LaVergne TN
LVHW041559070426
835507LV00011B/1191